· NORTHWEST ·

KNOW-HOW

HAUNTS

NORTHWEST
KNOW-HOW

HAUNTS

Bess Lovejoy

Illustrations by **Anarachel Humphrey**

SASQUATCH BOOKS
SEATTLE

Printed in China

SASQUATCH BOOKS with colophon is a registered trademark
of Penguin Random House LLC

26 25 24 23 22   9 8 7 6 5 4 3 2 1

Text: Bess Lovejoy
Illustrator: Anarachel Humphrey
Editor: Jennifer Worick
Production editor: Jill Saginario
Designer: Alicia Terry

Library of Congress Cataloging-in-Publication Data
Names: Lovejoy, Bess, author.
Title: Northwest know-how : haunts / Bess Lovejoy.
Other titles: Northwest knowhow, haunts
Identifiers: LCCN 2021021495 | ISBN 9781632174093 (hardcover)
Subjects: LCSH: Haunted places--Northwest, Pacific. | Ghosts--Northwest,
Pacific.
Classification: LCC BF1472.U6 L69 2022 | DDC 133.1/29795--dc23
LC record available at https://lccn.loc.gov/2021021495

ISBN: 978-1-63217-409-3

Sasquatch Books
1325 Fourth Avenue, Suite 1025
Seattle, WA 98101

SasquatchBooks.com

MIX
Paper from
responsible sources
FSC® C169962
www.fsc.org

Contents

1 WASHINGTON

PLUS . . .

OREGON

PLUS . . .

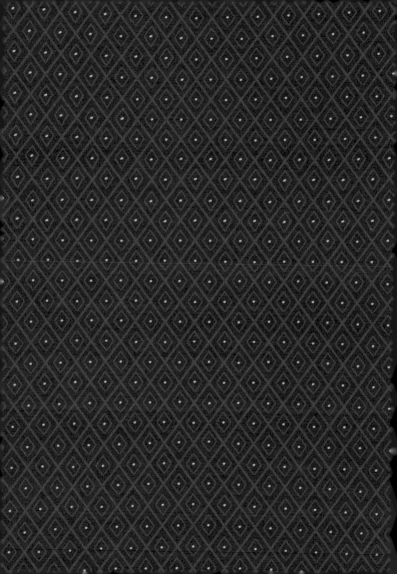

Acknowledgments

To the many folklorists, ghost hunters, and haunted history experts whose work I drew upon, including Athena, Ross Allison, Al Eufrasio, Jeff Davis, Jeff Dwyer, Mike Helm, Margaret Read MacDonald, Linda Moffitt, Donna Stewart, and others.

And to the frontline workers who gave their all during the COVID-19 pandemic while I sat in my apartment drinking tea and writing about ghosts.

Introduction

It's not unusual to hear the Pacific Northwest referred to as a dark place. We have a season called the Big Dark, after all, which runs roughly from October through "Juneuary." Grunge and other bleak musical subcultures have flourished here, beloved by generations of sodden, introverted types. We are, unfortunately, known for our serial killers. And then there are our ghosts.

All of America is a haunted place, but the ghosts of the Northwest have a special resonance. Our settler history began with the forced displacement (or worse) of Native American nations, and continued with risky, accident-prone industries such as logging, mining, and seafaring. Our earliest settlements could be crime-ridden—home to forced labor, smuggling, and exploitive sex work. All this generated intense emotions—fear, sadness, grief—which paranormal experts say can encourage hauntings. Some also think the water here acts as a ghostly conductor, bringing messages from other realms; in this sense, the rain is a spiritual fertilizer.

The surprise is that many Northwest ghosts are not all that dark. A number are friendly presences who watch over beloved former homes and businesses. There are certainly many sad stories too, but in this book, I have often chosen to favor tales that delight over those involving horrific crimes. (You won't find the usual serial killers here: they've gotten enough attention.) I've also usually avoided including buildings that are now private residences, out of respect for the living inhabitants.

It's worth noting that Washington and Oregon are home to thousands of reputedly ghostly locales, far more than we could include here. Think of this as a sampler platter of spirits—an amuse-bouche for the afterlife. If you're after more, consult the Resources on page 118 for ideas about how to find ghosts in your own backyard.

SEDRO-WOOLLEY
- Northern State Hospital

SEATTLE
- Butterworth Building
- Catalysis Corporation
- Comet Lodge Cemetery
- Georgetown Castle
- Mexican Consulate
- Pacific Tower
- Pier 70
- Pike Place Market
- Seattle Underground
- Smith Tower

PORT TOWNSEND
- Manresa Castle Hotel

PORT GAMBLE
- Walker-Ames House

TACOMA
- Old City Hall

LAKEWOOD
- Thornewood Castle

BLACK DIAMOND
- Ghost Town of Franklin

VANCOUVER
- Interstate 5 Bridge
- Slocum House

WASHINGTON

Seattle Underground

102 CHERRY STREET, SEATTLE

The founders of Seattle were ambitious and hardworking, but they weren't always brilliant engineers. The early city was constructed at sea level, and every high tide brought flooded streets and overflowing toilets. After a major fire blazed in 1889, city leaders rebuilt the town a story higher, leading to a system of elevated buildings alternating with sea-level sidewalks. Seventeen people died just trying to navigate the uneven streets. Eventually the whole city was raised, and the first-story structures were sealed in 1907 amid fears of plague-carrying rats (really).

Journalist Bill Speidel rediscovered the underground in the mid-twentieth century and began leading tours. Over the decades, subterranean guides and tourists have reported hearing strange noises and seeing phosphorescent outlines of the "seamstresses" (read: sex workers) so key to Seattle's early economy. The most haunted site is said to be an old bank vault beneath one of the amethyst-colored prism glass sidewalks where a gold rush–era miner and bank teller still lurk. They're rumored to be remnants of a murder meant to separate the miner from his gold—back when Seattle's streets were doubly dangerous.

Smith Tower

506 SECOND AVENUE, SEATTLE

A relic from a more elegant era, Smith Tower rises 462 feet from Seattle's historic core. That may not seem impressive now, but when the tower opened in 1914, it was both Seattle's first skyscraper and the tallest building west of the Mississippi.

Security guards have reported that the building's historic Otis elevators are frequently summoned to empty floors, and they've spotted mysterious dark silhouettes on their monitors. A female figure also roams the thirty-fifth-floor observatory and then vanishes right before their eyes. In the 1980s, a worker saw the ghost of an older woman creep up behind him while he was putting together some historical exhibits. Later shown a picture of Bertha Knight Landes—Seattle's first female mayor, who governed 1926–1928—he recognized the image as the figure who'd been peering over his shoulder, perhaps trying to check out his handiwork.

Pike Place Market

85 PIKE STREET, SEATTLE

The market is reportedly home to so many spooks it's basically a ghost general assembly. There are the two spirits who duke it out in the downstairs fridge of Mr. D's Greek Delicacies, a translucent little boy who throws beads at customers in the Bead Zone, and a World War II–era swing dancer who whirls in the Economy Building, to name just a few.

But the most frequently seen figure is a Native American woman who appears alive, at least until you realize her feet aren't touching the floor. Some identify her as Princess Angeline, the eldest daughter of Chief Si'ahl (also known as Chief Seattle), who was born around 1820 and originally named Kikisoblu. When the Duwamish were sent to live on reservations, Kikisoblu remained, living in a shack on Western Avenue and selling handicrafts. Today, tourists see her sitting on the market floor near the flower sellers, only to discover that she's disappeared once they've decided to buy something. When they ask a flower vendor about her, they're told, "Oh, that was Princess Angeline." Out-of-towners look confused, while in-the-know locals turn very, very pale.

Butterworth Building

1921 FIRST AVENUE, SEATTLE

E. R. Butterworth opened Seattle's first building exclusively for mortuary services in 1903. The funeral home attended to many of the city's most prominent families, but also served one of the city's most notorious quacks: "Doctor" Linda Hazzard, who sent some of her victims there to be cremated after they starved to death at her sanitarium in Olalla. (The Butterworths themselves were never convicted of any wrongdoing.)

The top floor has been home to a series of restaurants, but most don't stay for long. Visitors report a ghostly male presence in the women's bathroom, silverware that slides off tables, candles that burst into flame, wine bottles that explode, and funereal singing. Cooks, electricians, and other workers have been known to leave the premises midtask after seeing things they can't possibly explain.

Kells Irish Restaurant & Bar, on the ground floor, has managed to stay in the building since the 1980s, despite disembodied voices and mirrors that shatter for no reason. Perhaps the ghosts there are friendlier—one of their most famous spirits is a little redheaded girl who calls children to play and gives them a (very real) rag doll.

Pier 70

2801 ALASKAN WAY, SEATTLE

Sometimes ghosts just want to help. At Seattle's Pier 70, built in 1902 to handle salmon boats but since remodeled to hold offices, shops, and restaurants, employees report sightings of a ghostly sailor in a peacoat and slouched hat. "Paddy" usually appears at closing time, seen in a mirror or out of the corner of one's eyes. He's most famous for appearing to those who come to the pier depressed and thinking of ending their lives. Paddy talks to them, convincing them that life is worth living. He doesn't stick around to be thanked, vanishing once the person feels better.

Several people also claim to have seen a ghost ship out in Elliott Bay near the pier. Seeing the ghost ship is not a good sign, however— supposedly it foretells doom. So if you visit, keep your eyes off the water, and peeled for Paddy instead.

HAUNTED WASHINGTON PARKS

Green Lake

GREEN LAKE DRIVE N, SEATTLE

Few of the Seattleites who adore Green Lake know that it holds a sad secret. On June 17, 1926, a carpenter found first the shoes, then the body, of twenty-two-year-old Sylvia Gaines. Gaines had come to Seattle months earlier hoping to connect with her father, Bob, a WWI veteran who had split from her mother years ago. The resulting trial found evidence that Sylvia and her father had "unnatural relations" and that he'd killed her in a jealous rage. Bob Gaines was hanged in Walla Walla in 1928 for Sylvia's death. Today, people report the translucent figure of a young woman walking the trails, sobbing.

Fort Worden Historical State Park

BATTERY WAY, PORT TOWNSEND

Once an active military base, Fort Worden was built at the start of the twentieth century as part of the "Triangle of Fire," three forts guarding Puget Sound from naval invasion. For a century, people have reported weird goings-on there, especially at Building 298, once the military hospital. About 10:30 each night, a strange woman appears in the second-story window with a glowing light behind her.

Luna Park

ALKI BEACH PARK, 37 ALKI TRAIL, SEATTLE

Once a fantastic amusement park nicknamed the "Coney Island of the West," Luna Park once stood at the tip of Alki Beach Park. Home to roller coasters, live music, bathing pools, and the best-stocked bar in town, it was so bright it was visible from downtown Seattle. The park closed its doors in 1913 after a series of scandals, but the bathing pools lasted until a 1933 fire. These days, on the anniversary of the fire—April 14—people in downtown Seattle sometimes see a ghostly blaze where Luna Park once stood. They'll call the fire department, but no flames are ever found.

Catalysis Corporation

1601 E JOHN STREET, SEATTLE

The Reverend Daniel Bagley never actually preached at the Capitol Hill United Methodist Church, dying the year before the beautiful stained-glass-and-granite building was constructed in 1906. Nevertheless, the Seattle pioneer may be keeping an eye on the congregation he founded in the 1860s. Later pastors and other congregants have seen a transparent Bagley on the building's balcony, stairs, or bell tower, watching them. Sometimes, he's missing his legs. His wife, Susannah Bagley, also appears in a diaphanous form, bathed in blue light and floating near the ceiling. She asked at least one startled onlooker, "How do I get out?" before drifting off in the opposite direction.

The congregation left the church in 1991 when it was badly in need of repairs, and the building is now home to an advertising agency called Catalysis. Employees have said they sometimes hear organ music, the echoes of sermons, and snatches of a church choir that's long since left the building.

HAUNTED WASHINGTON THEATERS

Paramount Theatre

911 PINE STREET, SEATTLE

This luxurious landmark has a ghost that employees have nicknamed "Erie." The story goes that when he was alive, Erie enjoyed going on theater dates with his wife. After his death, she continued the dates, always buying the seat next to her and behaving as if her husband was still present. Her friends thought she'd lost touch with reality, but others sense that Erie is still around to enjoy his dates even in the afterlife.

Neptune Theatre

1303 NE FORTY-FIFTH STREET, SEATTLE

The spectral images spotted at this venerable U-District theater include a screaming blue face birthing itself from a wall (à la *Alien*) and a woman in a black gown who hovers several inches off the ground. At least one janitor used to summon a grayish female ghost whose cold spot functioned as an air-conditioner while he worked.

Fox Theatre

123 S TOWER AVENUE, CENTRALIA

This Art Deco gem, once the biggest theater between Portland and Tacoma, has a history of spooky disturbances. There are reports of a ghostly usher near the women's bathroom on the mezzanine, and poltergeist activity along stairs on the same floor. Paranormal investigators from AGHOST also saw shadowy figures, felt something circling them, and smelled a strange perfume.

Capitol Theatre

19 S THIRD STREET, YAKIMA

"Shorty" is the name of the resident ghost here. He opens and closes doors, makes the spotlights dance, and even leaves footprints in the dust. (He causes particular disturbances at rock concerts, which he dislikes.) Shorty also once saved a girl's life by making a piece of plaster falling from the ceiling move sideways.

Kelso Theater Pub

214 S PACIFIC AVENUE, KELSO

Paranormal researchers have had a field day here, and once apparently captured a male spirit saying, "I'm sure I am dead," on an audio recording.

Mount Baker Theatre

104 N COMMERCIAL STREET #4408, BELLINGHAM

Often cited as one of the most haunted places in the state, this luxurious movie palace is watched over by a ghost named Judy, who develops "crushes" on male projectionists and calls out their names. She's even been captured in a photo—assuming it's her in all that white mist. Some sensitives have also seen the spirit of a large black cat, which researchers trace to a circus that visited in the 1930s and that brought along an ailing panther.

Pacific Tower

1200 TWELFTH AVENUE S, SEATTLE

It's hard to miss at night when this striking Art Deco building looms out of the mist atop Beacon Hill. Depending on your history in Seattle, you might know it as office space, the former headquarters of Amazon.com, or the US Marine Hospital. That facility, which opened in 1933, served veterans, the Coast Guard, lighthouse keepers, and the poor for decades before becoming the Seattle Public Health Service Hospital.

Dot-commers and others working in the tower have described being followed through the hallways by what sounds like a squeaking hospital gurney. When they turn around, the noise stops, only to start back up again as they continue walking. Janitors have run out of the building after witnessing objects levitating off desks. But the most famous ghost is a nurse who isn't seen so much as smelled. She wears a heavy rose-scented perfume and calls for people to wait for her. It's not clear if she thinks she's spotted a fellow hospital staff member, or if she thinks you're a patient she wants to take care of one last time.

Monaghan Mansion, Gonzaga University

502 E BOONE AVENUE, SPOKANE

Organ music wafting from empty rooms. Notes playing on a phantom flute. Smells of sulfur, and worse. Snarling from the basement, and the sudden sensation of being strangled. All were reported at Gonzaga's Monaghan Mansion—home to the school's music department—in late 1974 and 1975. Six sets of exorcism prayers finally quelled whatever unclean spirit had taken up residence, but some say the place still retains an uneasy aura.

Everett High School

2416 COLBY AVENUE, EVERETT

This beautiful beaux arts building is home to stories of a "Blue Ghost" in the auditorium. Supposedly, a worker renovating the site many years ago fell through some plasterboard on the ceiling and died after breaking his neck on the seats. Students and staff have reported strange glows, a spotlight that follows them around, seats banging down, and cold blasts of air when the auditorium is supposedly empty.

University of Puget Sound

1500 N WARNER STREET, TACOMA

The small Norton Clapp Theatre here is home to some kind of spirit that moves around scenery and makes unearthly noises. But it can be a friendly ghost too: One student who lost her balance on the catwalk and began to fall felt a helpful force pulling her back up.

Georgetown Castle

6420 CARLETON AVENUE S, SEATTLE

The Georgetown "Castle" is merely a Victorian-era house painted in melon shades, with a turret and a gargoyle perched in the garden. But if the architecture isn't so unusual, its history and legends certainly are. Built in 1902 by Peter Gessner, owner of Pioneer Square's Central Tavern, the house originally served as a gambling saloon and brothel—part of a red-light district so scarlet one reverend called it "the cesspool of Seattle."

Gessner lived in the house less than a year before ending his life by drinking carbolic acid. The place later became a rooming house, clubhouse, and possibly the site of illegal abortions performed by a doctor who owned the house in the 1910s. In the 1970s, its owners frequently saw the ghost of a tall, thin older woman in Victorian dress with eyes "like burning coal." The ghost told one of the owners her name was Sarah, and convinced him to paint her portrait. Over the years, she showed herself to dozens of guests, sometimes appearing near the apparition of a threatening-looking man while clutching her throat. Yet Sarah is mostly kind: Once she even rolled a loaf of bread down the counter to a visitor who wanted a midnight snack. If you want to experience Sarah for yourself, please note this is a private residence; however, it's occasionally open as part of home and garden tours.

Mexican Consulate

807 E ROY STREET, SEATTLE

This beloved Capitol Hill building with its emerald-green trim was the Harvard Exit Theatre from 1969 until 2015. Before that, it was the Women's Century Club, and it seems the suffragettes stuck around. In the 1970s, the theater manager repeatedly witnessed the fireplace burning and the lobby chairs drawn into a circle when she opened up in the morning, as if a club meeting had been held overnight. Projectors also ran on their own, and film canisters moved or disappeared. Some people have also seen an apparition of a woman dressed in Victorian clothing wandering the halls.

John S. McMillin Memorial Mausoleum

664 AFTERGLOW DRIVE, FRIDAY HARBOR, SAN JUAN ISLAND

Hike an overgrown path through the woods near Roche Harbor (look for the signs saying "Afterglow Vista") and you'll come upon one of the most interesting funerary monuments in the United States. John S. McMillin, owner of the local lime works, had a unique personal philosophy and wanted a tomb that would express his views. The centerpiece is a limestone table surrounded by chairs, one for each McMillin family member and arranged in the same spot as they sat at the dinner table. Beneath the chairs are their ashes. As the sun sets on summer evenings, some say you can see ghostly outlines of the family having dinner together once again.

Lake View Cemetery

1554 FIFTEENTH AVENUE E, SEATTLE

One of the highest points in the city, Lake View is a great spot for beautiful views of the Cascade and Olympic Mountains as well as Lake Washington. If you're very lucky, you might also catch a glimpse of the cemetery's more ethereal occupants, including an iridescent ghost horse who clomps along the cement paths at night. (Yes, the horse—named Buck—was buried at the cemetery, although perhaps only briefly.)

Black Diamond Cemetery

CEMETERY HILL ROAD, BLACK DIAMOND

On the National Register of Historic Places, the Black Diamond Cemetery is the final home for dozens of immigrants who died in local mining disasters and children who perished in epidemics. Supposedly, on foggy nights you can still hear miners whistling and see the red glow from their lanterns. You might also see a mysterious woman searching among the tombstones—for the grave of a lost lover or child, no one is quite sure.

Comet Lodge Cemetery

2100 S GRAHAM STREET, SEATTLE

A quiet corner of Beacon Hill just off I-5 is home to a story straight from a horror movie, except it's all real. The Comet Lodge Cemetery was originally a Duwamish burial ground and became a cemetery for some of Seattle's earliest settlers by the 1880s. In its prime, it was home to about eight hundred graves. The last recorded burial was in 1936, after which it fell into disrepair. In the 1980s, much of the cemetery was bulldozed and sold for redevelopment, including the area reserved for child burials.

While the tombstones were moved, it's less clear where the bodies went. Residents in nearby homes have reported repeated hauntings, including specters of children dressed in clothes from the early 1900s who appear to their own living children at night. People who visit what's left of the cemetery report the sound of children laughing, and some have seen a ghostly little boy who wanders the small patch of remaining graves, perhaps looking for a final resting place that turned out to be not so final after all.

HAUNTED WASHINGTON HOTELS

Hotel Sorrento

900 MADISON STREET, SEATTLE

At the Sorrento's bar, wineglasses move without human hands and ghostly footsteps resound through empty halls. Most stories come from the fourth floor, however, where a transparent woman flits to room 408 and then vanishes. Some say it's Alice B. Toklas, Gertrude Stein's partner, whose childhood home was nearby.

Lake Quinault Lodge

345 S SHORE ROAD, QUINAULT

This graceful lodge inside the Olympic National Park is haunted by the ghost of a devoted front desk employee named Beverley, who came to work despite feeling ill one day in 1924 and died tragically when a fire broke out. Beverley is a prankster who loves music; she switches on the radios and plays piano in the wee hours. At least one guest who went to investigate the tunes said that as he approached, he saw her ghost running away down the hall.

Bush House Inn

308 FIFTH STREET, INDEX

This last hotel and restaurant in Index, once a thriving mining town of the 1880s, is rumored to have been built over graves. The most famous story here is of a woman who took her own life after hearing that her husband had died in a mining accident. Alas, the story wasn't true, and she now haunts room nine.

Mount Baker Hotel

45951 MAIN STREET, CONCRETE

If you visit this hotel, originally built in 1924 to house dam construction workers, be sure to check out the main floor. It was once home to a cafe where the apparition of a woman dressed in 1940s clothing sometimes appears near an antique phonograph, and where the ghost of a soldier killed in Vietnam is known to turn up.

Rosario Resort

1400 ROSARIO ROAD, EASTSOUND

The story goes that former Moran Mansion owner Donald Rheem brought his wife, Alice, here in the 1930s to curb her drinking and flirting. It didn't work. Alice zoomed around Orcas Island on a motorcycle in a red negligee and brought handsome soldiers over when her husband was away. Employees still see and feel her, and guests hear suggestive noises in empty bedrooms.

Tokeland Hotel

2964 KINDRED AVENUE, TOKELAND

Guests here feel a ghost cat who jumps on their beds and see the imprint of little human feet on their sheets. The latter are thought to be from the son of a former owner who died after getting stuck in the mud of the bay. There are also unexplained flashes of light, weird raps, and a sense of being watched that comes over guests and paranormal investigators alike.

Ghost Town of Franklin

NEAR BLACK DIAMOND

The former site of Franklin is home to one of the state's worst mining disasters, when thirty-seven coal miners perished in a horrific fire in 1894. Today, only ruins are left: an old mining cart, a covered mining shaft, and a tiny cemetery choked by black-berry brambles.

Strange things happen in the area at night—weird shadows, lights like those from old lanterns, and the sounds of horse-drawn wagons reverberate through the hills. Some say if you hurl rocks down the shaft, you hear the screams of dead miners rising back up.

Old City Hall

625 COMMERCE STREET, TACOMA

Many of the stories about Tacoma's Old City Hall concern the bells, which were donated in 1904 by prominent citizen (and later ambassador to France) Hugh Wallace in honor of his daughter Mildred, who died at age twelve in 1903.

The lights in the bell tower have been known to turn on and off on their own, and the bells ring even when the striking apparatus is disconnected. This happened so often that a few decades ago, a building manager, Jim Brewster, spent the night to see what was going on. The bells stayed quiet, but Brewster sensed an inhuman presence.

The building has since been used for many other purposes, including several restaurants. While the Tacoma Bar & Grill was there, staff experienced a poltergeist they nicknamed "Gus." He liked to shatter wineglasses, sweep bottles off shelves, and turn off the stove, but you only had to holler his name to make it stop.

Oxford Saloon

913 FIRST STREET, SNOHOMISH

Built in 1900 as a dry-goods store, the Oxford is also said to have once been a high-class bordello. Some of the prostitutes may remain in the building, alongside a madame attired in purple. Henry, the ghost of a policeman killed in a bar fight, also shows up. He haunts the basement stairs and women's restrooms, where he pinches people or whispers, "Get out!"

Colophon Cafe

1208 ELEVENTH STREET, BELLINGHAM

Just about every building in Fairhaven is reportedly haunted;
the area is even home to a phantom freight train that appears
each December 21, the anniversary of a railroad disaster. This
cozy restaurant is said to be inhabited by a spirit who likes
to rearrange glasses, silverware, and condiments, and to
move parts of meals around the kitchen. (Staff swear they
are innocent.)

Merchants Cafe

109 YESLER WAY, SEATTLE

Built in 1890, this is one of the oldest restaurants in Seattle
and once had a brothel upstairs. A painting on a back wall is
said to depict a "seamstress" who now haunts the top floors.
Bartenders have seen patrons suddenly vanish, and people in
the upper-floor apartments sometimes feel ghostly presences
crawling into bed with them.

Canterbury Ale House

534 FIFTEENTH AVENUE E, SEATTLE

The Canterbury, as locals call it, is home to a haunted mirror.
Peer into the glass near the fireplace and you might see the
reflection of a man looking down. Glance back into the bar,
however, and you'll notice the man isn't there at all. Legend
has it that if you look into the mirror for long enough, the man
will eventually look up at you—only to reveal a gaping hole
where his face should be.

Central Club & Tavern

124 KIRKLAND AVENUE, KIRKLAND

Open since the 1930s, this dive bar (okay, technically not an
eatery) is a Kirkland institution. Newspaper clippings and photos
line the walls, plus kitsch including a stuffed armadillo. A few
patrons and employees say that on slow nights or after closing,
a glowing "pink lady" has appeared at the back of the building.

Billy's Bar & Grill

322 E HERON STREET, ABERDEEN

Billy Gohl has been blamed for dozens of deaths, allegedly robbing and murdering so many sailors and workers from 1906–1909 that he's been called the "Ghoul of Grays Harbor." The "floater fleet" of decomposing corpses that used to surface in nearby waterways? Billy's doing—allegedly. More recently, Saint Martin's University history professor and Aberdeen native Aaron Goings has recast Gohl—a powerful agent for the Sailors' Union of the Pacific—as the victim of local businesses who framed him for trying to end lumber trade abuses. Either way, patrons at the bar Billy once ran have reported chills, a strange fog on the mirror, and a cold-faced bartender who disappears when approached.

Thornewood Castle

8601 N THORNE LANE SW, LAKEWOOD

Chester Thorne was one of the most successful financiers around Puget Sound at the start of the twentieth century. He spent more than $1 million to build this Tudor Gothic mansion, using parts from an Elizabethan manor in England that he had shipped over piece by piece. The mansion was completed in 1911, and Thorne lived here with his family until he died in 1927.

Yet Chester never really left, later owners of the estate say. He reportedly likes to unscrew light bulbs to get people's attention, among other little tricks. His wife, Anna, has also been seen, especially by brides who rent the castle for their weddings and spot her in a vintage mirror while preparing for their big day.

Former owners have also experienced the sounds of ghostly cocktail parties, smelled hints of leather and perfume, and watched a couple in strange outfits materialize on a staircase. The castle was used as a film location for the 2002 Stephen King miniseries *Rose Red*, but rest assured the ghosts in *that* haunted mansion are purely fictional.

Manresa Castle Hotel

651 CLEVELAND STREET, PORT TOWNSEND

An undead monk in the attic is a trope that might seem better suited to Gothic novels, but some say that's one of the spirits haunting this Port Townsend hotel. Completed in 1892 as the home for prominent local businessman Charles Eisenbeis, the place became a training college for Jesuit priests in the 1920s. (They named the building Manresa Hall after the town in Spain where their order was founded.) In 1968, the site was converted into a hotel.

A monk (or priest, stories differ) is said to have hanged himself in the attic, and some still feel his unhappy presence. A young woman named Kate is also said to have thrown herself from an upstairs window after learning that her lover was lost at sea. There's no documentary proof of either of these stories, but they've made the rounds for decades to explain odd goings-on at the place. Guests and employees here feel cold spots, see glasses shatter, and hear voices whispering their name. One woman saw a translucent apparition that lasted for several seconds, accompanied by the powerful stench of decay.

Walker-Ames House

Port Gamble was built as a company town for workers in the local mill in the 1850s, and the place has an eerie, empty New England quality to it. If you're looking for the most haunted house in the most haunted town in Washington, this might be it.

The ornate Walker-Ames House, built for the mill's lead mechanic, has been empty for decades except for occasional tours. People frequently see the faces of a nanny or children peering out of the attic windows, and some have experienced a disturbed little boy in the basement—possibly the ghost of a child who was once locked away. Paranormal researchers have seen a female shadow that manifests in a closet, and often feel suddenly sick in a bathroom nearby. Some claim to have snapped photos of ghostly figures, captured audio of disembodied voices, and even seen strange messages scrawled on the windows.

Northern State Hospital

25625 HELMICK ROAD, SEDRO-WOOLLEY

Northern State, one of several state-run asylums for the mentally ill in the twentieth century, once held as many as 2,700 people. Some of them were given electric-shock treatments and transorbital lobotomies. Many committed were not actually mentally ill: they were immigrants, epileptics, menopausal women, alcoholics, or just people who had trouble fitting into mainstream society. Yet compared to some other asylums, Northern State had a reputation for being relatively humane, with beautiful grounds and a dairy farm and canning operation that served as occupational therapy.

Abandoned since 1973, many of the decaying buildings are now part of a recreation area. Some see the spirit of a little girl bouncing a red ball, and a man who seems to follow her. People have also seen weird shadows and lights, heard voices whispering in the nurse's dorms, and seen objects fly right off shelves. One of the most frightening apparitions is of a dead nurse seen hanging from a noose. Northern State is also known as a place that can produce ghostly photos: in 2006, one paranormal investigator captured an image of a person standing in a tunnel when there wasn't anyone (living) there.

Slocum House

605 ESTHER STREET, VANCOUVER

Built in 1867 for merchant Charles Slocum, this two-story Italianate home has also served as a popular theater, a winery, and now an event venue. There's a male presence—possibly Charles Slocum himself—who sometimes creates annoying sounds and menacing energy, particularly in the basement. A female spirit also appears as a cloudlike mist, especially when children's plays or parties are held. It's said that Laura Slocum, Charles's wife, was very fond of children and liked to invite them to the house for parties and cookies. Some researchers think the presence of children in the house may be prompting Laura to come back for one last gathering.

Interstate 5 Bridge

VANCOUVER, WA

One cool, drizzly October Sunday in 1920, G. R. Percival went walking. His wife thought little of it: Her husband, Vancouver's mayor, was prone to taking long walks to clear his head. But when he failed to return that evening, she got worried.

The next day, downtown businesses closed at 1 p.m. as 300 men searched the city. The Columbia River was dragged three times, and bulletins circulated up and down the West Coast. Witnesses said they'd seen the mayor walking over the Interstate Bridge toward Portland, then walking back to the city he governed. But no one had seen him since that Sunday.

That is, until a Portlander named O. F. Williams discovered Percival's body hanging from a tree on Hayden Island in November. Despite weeks of decomposition, his body was easily identified thanks to his watch, papers, and the signet ring that still clung to one of his fingers. The death was ruled a suicide, although some questions linger.

These days, on some misty autumn evenings, people see a tall, well-dressed man in an overcoat walking the old interstate bridge. He appears normal enough, apart from his out-of-date clothing, but has a tendency to disappear into the darkness, just like the mayor disappeared that Sunday in 1920.

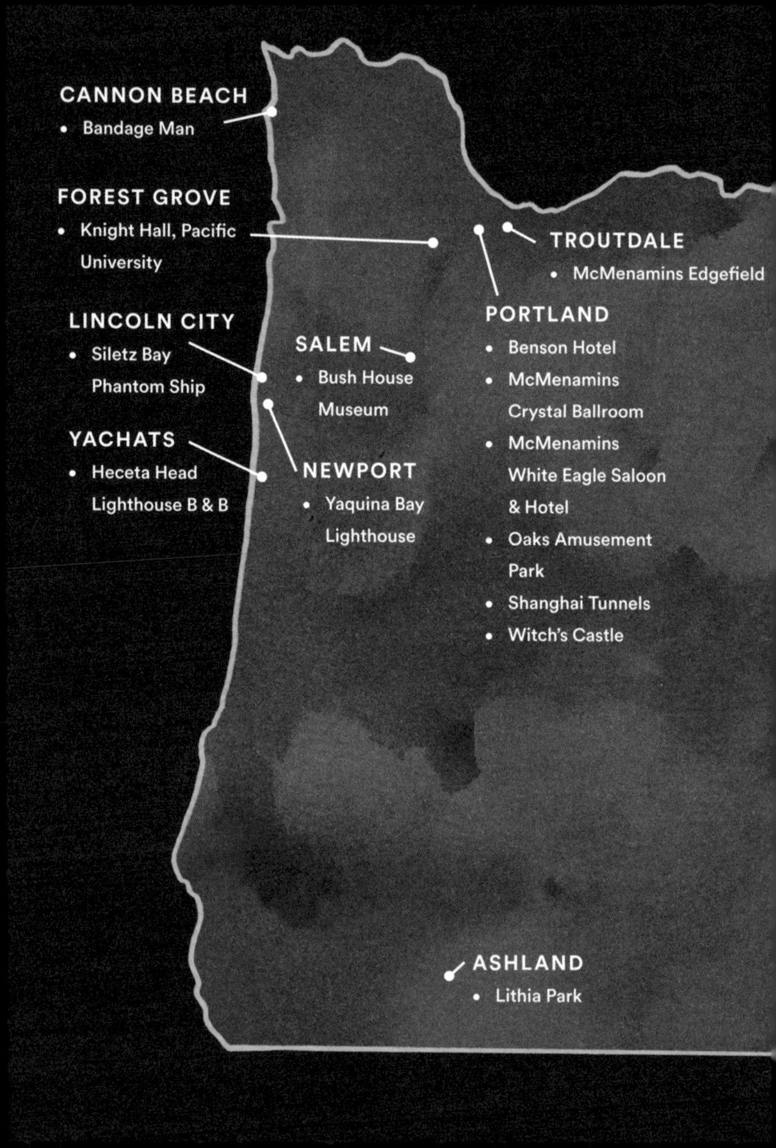

CANNON BEACH
- Bandage Man

FOREST GROVE
- Knight Hall, Pacific University

LINCOLN CITY
- Siletz Bay Phantom Ship

YACHATS
- Heceta Head Lighthouse B & B

SALEM
- Bush House Museum

NEWPORT
- Yaquina Bay Lighthouse

TROUTDALE
- McMenamins Edgefield

PORTLAND
- Benson Hotel
- McMenamins Crystal Ballroom
- McMenamins White Eagle Saloon & Hotel
- Oaks Amusement Park
- Shanghai Tunnels
- Witch's Castle

ASHLAND
- Lithia Park

LA GRANDE

- The Lodge at Hot
  Lake Springs

OREGON

ONTARIO

- Malheur Butte

Shanghai Tunnels

SAID TO BE BELOW OLD TOWN
CHINATOWN, PORTLAND

Paranormal guidebooks and television shows tell a ghastly tale of what happened in the Shanghai Tunnels. Men who wandered West in search of work in the logging industry or to find their fortunes in the goldfields were drugged, dropped through trapdoors in bars, kept in dank holding cells, and smuggled through underground passageways before being sold to sea captains on the waterfront who were desperate for crew members. By the time they woke up from their stupor, these "shanghaied" men were on ships bound for lucrative trading ports of the East.

The tunnels connecting the waterfront to other parts of Portland also allegedly hosted prostitutes, opium dens, and other unsavory activities. There's a problem, though: most historians say these tunnels never existed. Men *were* shanghaied in ports along the West Coast, but any passageways beneath Portland connected only a few businesses at a time. Nevertheless, tourists in the "tunnels" (really basements) beneath the city report intense fear and anguish, disembodied cries, and wet hands on their shoulders—perhaps the spirits of kidnapped sailors looking for revenge?

Benson Hotel

309 SW BROADWAY, PORTLAND

The Benson Hotel, which opened in 1913, is known for luxurious touches like Austrian crystal chandeliers, Italian marble floors, and a lobby paneled with walnut sourced from the forests of Imperial Russia. The place was the pride and joy of Simon Benson, a Norwegian immigrant turned successful lumber baron and Portland philanthropist. (One of Benson's most notable efforts was donating twenty bronze drinking fountains to the city; they were nicknamed Benson Bubblers.)

Some say Benson remains at his hotel. He's been spotted slowly descending the staircase into the lobby and wandering through the lounge. A noted teetotaler, he scowls at guests drinking alcohol. If the scowl doesn't work, he's been known to knock over a martini or two.

Benson is just one of five spirits guests have spotted. There's also a friendly porter who helps people get into bed; a little boy of about three who pulls scary faces; a Lady in White who traipses the floors admiring the decor; and a Lady in Blue, who wears a turquoise dress and red rings. She often appears as a reflection in mirrors, and disappears in an instant if spoken to.

McMenamins Crystal Ballroom

1332 W BURNSIDE STREET, PORTLAND

There are a limited number of places in the world that can boast jitterbugging ghosts, but Portland's Crystal Ballroom is one of them. Opened in 1914 as the Cotillion Hall, it's seen a century that included square dancing and apple cider, major music acts like Little Richard and James Brown, neglect and abandonment, and finally revitalization starting in 1997 thanks to the McMenamin brothers, who specialize in saving local historic properties from doom.

Staff at the Crystal Ballroom have seen men and women in '20s and '30s garb twirling and kicking as they dance the jitterbug along the ballroom's famous "floating floor." Employees have also heard the squeak of shoe leather and the sounds of people laughing, talking, and partying when the building is otherwise empty. Psychics theorize that the intense joy the place has seen over the years has accreted in the walls, absorbed by the minerals in the bricks only to be "replayed" later in a phantom party that never ends.

HAUNTED OREGON CEMETERIES

Lone Fir Cemetery

649 SE TWENTY-SIXTH AVENUE, PORTLAND

How could Lone Fir not be haunted? It's home to more than 25,000 graves, at least 10,000 of those unknown and unmarked thanks to poor record-keeping. People get weird feelings here—cold columns of air and the sense that they shouldn't get too close to certain monuments. A section known as Hawthorn's Plot, for Dr. James C. Hawthorne (founder of Oregon's first insane asylum) creates especially eerie vibes. Hundreds of his patients, many abandoned by their families, are buried here alongside him.

There's also at least one report of a screaming, zombie-like figure in the cemetery, as well as more pleasant encounters with a spectral woman in a red dress who seems happy as she strolls the grounds.

Salem Pioneer Cemetery

COMMERCIAL STREET SE & HOYT STREET SE, SALEM

Many notable pioneers are buried here, including well-known local undertaker William Graves (yes, really). His grave has been lost, and his spirit is said to walk the place at night. People have also heard a clanging lantern and encountered an angry ghost who yells from behind a monument—possibly Graves himself.

Jacksonville Cemetery

CEMETERY ROAD, JACKSONVILLE

One of the oldest and biggest historic cemeteries in Oregon (official burials go back to 1859), this place has reports of hooded figures lurking among the tombstones and strange green mists.

McMenamins White Eagle Saloon & Hotel

836 N RUSSELL STREET, PORTLAND

If you're looking for the most haunted place to drink in Portland, consider the White Eagle.

Many of the stories here surround an early-twentieth-century second-floor brothel and a sex worker named Rose who was the owner's favorite. Legend has it that Rose was murdered by a piano player who had fallen in love with her and who tried, but failed, to take her away to Seattle. Guests hear strange sobbing and see the apparition of a young, pretty woman roaming the halls. Some even report being propositioned by a misty figure once they crawl into a bed.

Other stories concern a man named Sam who worked as a cook and lived upstairs. By some accounts, Sam was abandoned at the place as a child and, after many years, died in his upstairs room. Guests who use the central restroom in the middle of the night sometimes come face-to-face with him, realizing with a start that the weary old man they're looking at is totally see-through.

HAUNTED OREGON THEATERS

Elsinore Theatre

170 HIGH STREET SE, SALEM

This 1926 Tudor Gothic venue is said to have a spot on stage that's so frigid it raises all the hair on the back of your neck. There are also blood splatters in the bathroom that appear and disappear, and a man in a suit who walks right through the seating.

Allen Elizabethan Theatre

15 S PIONEER STREET, ASHLAND

This open-sky theater has been home to the Oregon Shakespeare Festival for decades, and it may also be home to one soul who never made it for curtain-up, at least while alive. The story goes that British actor Charles Laughton was due to appear in the 1962 summer festival but died before he could arrive. People have heard his laugh resounding through the theater on opening night, and many claim to have heard or seen him since.

Liberty Theatre

1203 COMMERCIAL STREET, ASTORIA

A ghostly couple named Paul and Mary haunts the second-floor restroom of this beautifully restored landmark, causing intense cold spots and creepy sensations. Mary also appears, dressed in early-twentieth-century clothing, in a mirror. Another ghost named Lily haunts the main-floor back-row seat where she died, generating what the author Jeff Dwyer calls a "cold cell of sadness."

Linkville Playhouse

201 MAIN STREET, KLAMATH FALLS

"Ralph," a former actor at this theater, is said to stick around in spectral form, playing music and smoking a pipe. He sometimes shows up during dress rehearsals, only to suddenly vanish.

Bijou Theatre

1624 NE HIGHWAY 101, LINCOLN CITY

The ghost at this 1930s movie theater enjoys organ music. In 2000, a man was playing the organ in preparation for a silent film fest when he saw a woman, glowing and all in white, hovering near the seats and then zooming toward him. When the music stopped, she disappeared.

Hollywood Theatre

4122 NE SANDY BOULEVARD, PORTLAND

If you visit this luxurious 1920s-era movie palace, don't be
startled if you feel a tap on your back or a whisper in your ear.
A male ghost—perhaps a former vaudeville performer—is said
to enjoy doing both, but he doesn't mean any harm. There are
also reports of a middle-aged man who hovers in the lobby,
and a blonde in high heels who paces the halls while smoking.

Heceta Head Lighthouse B & B

92072 HIGHWAY 101 SOUTH, YACHATS

Built on a rocky headland far above the sea, the lighthouse at Heceta Head is one of the most photographed in the nation. Yet the stories here swirl not around the tower itself but the assistant keeper's cottage, said to be home to the spirit of a long-dead woman named Rue.

Tales of Rue date back to the 1970s, when Lane Community College owned the place. The most famous story concerns a worker who was in the attic fixing a broken window when he came face-to-face with an old woman dressed in a gray gown. She floated toward him about six inches off the ground, then turned transparent and sailed through his body.

That night, when the attic should have been empty, the caretakers heard the sounds of sweeping and the tinkle of broken glass. When they went up later, the glass from the shattered window had been swept into a perfect pile.

Some say Rue is a lighthouse keeper's wife searching for her child's grave. Indeed, the baby daughter of the first keeper here died (possibly of scarlet fever) due to a lack of prompt medical attention. The grave is said to be somewhere on-site, but has long since disappeared in the tangle of blackberry bushes.

HAUNTED OREGON PARKS

Lotus Isle Park

N TOMAHAWK ISLAND DRIVE, PORTLAND

One of the weirder stories in Portland history (and that's saying something), Lotus Isle was apparently an attempt to shake down another nearby amusement park, Jantzen Beach on Hayden Island. But the Jantzen folks, of swimwear fame, were magnanimous or smart enough to say there was plenty of room for everyone. Lotus Isle thrilled Portlanders from 1930–1932 until a child's accidental death, an investor's suicide, a plane crash, and a fire ended the place. Today, people report the hubbub of spectral crowds and the sound of long-gone roller coasters.

Pioneer Park

400 NW DESPAIN AVENUE, PENDLETON

Not many children's playgrounds are also pioneer graveyards, but parents here don't seem to mind too much. There are at least thirteen old graves here, and possibly more. Some visitors say they feel watched, and hear footsteps when no one's around. There have also been suspicious fires on the play equipment. Not surprisingly, some speculate the ghosts aren't too happy about sharing eternal rest with the kiddos.

Lithia Park

WINBURN WAY, ASHLAND

If you drive through Lithia Park at night, look out for a sapphire-colored light that flickers like a flame. Said to favor the duck ponds, it's rumored to be the ghost of a girl murdered in the park in 1875. A group who drove through the light in 1975 reported a "sharp, damp coldness," according to the writer Donna Stewart.

Two other park legends are even odder. One concerns a 1920s "dog-faced boy" who suffered from hypertrichosis, a medical condition that causes excessive hair growth. Without parental support, he sold pencils on street corners and stole from unlocked vehicles. He disappeared in 1926, but four decades later, reports of a dog-faced boy stealing in the park cropped up again. He seemed impossible to capture, and some theorized the crimes were caused by the ghost of the original dog-faced child.

Then there's the musical guardian logger. Legend has it that a big, kindhearted logger was crushed to death by a falling tree in the park in the 1940s. He now watches out for others, pushing or pulling them away just as a tree falls. As they're saved, people hear music played on an old drinking jug—the dead logger's favorite pastime.

HAUNTED
OREGON
HOTELS

Columbia Gorge Hotel

4000 WESTCLIFF DRIVE, HOOD RIVER

Reports of paranormal activity here are mostly associated with the honeymoon suite and the third floor, where fires start by themselves and furniture suddenly barricades empty rooms. One person reported seeing a dark-haired young woman leap from the hotel tower. The apparition didn't land, but vanished in midair.

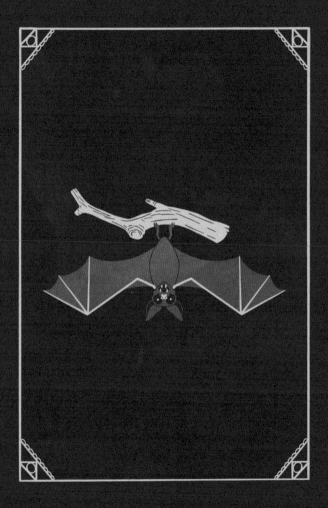

Wolf Creek Inn & Tavern

100 FRONT STREET, WOLF CREEK

Built in 1883, the Wolf Creek Inn claims to be the oldest continually operated hotel in the Pacific Northwest. Some say they've smelled cigar smoke near the Clark Gable suite or seen Jack London's reflection in a second-floor mirror (both men were once guests). But the hotel is known for something even stranger: a vampiric, bat-like being that prowls around the property dripping blood.

McMenamins Grand Lodge

3505 PACIFIC AVENUE, FOREST GROVE

This former Masonic and Eastern Star Home for the aged is known for its Lavender Lady. Construction crews working there in 1999 reported bursts of lavender fragrance, and one worker saw a white-haired woman dance from a hallway to a bathroom, leaving the herbal scent in her wake. Today, her likeness is painted on one of the hotel's walls.

Old Wheeler Hotel

495 HIGHWAY 101, WHEELER

Built in 1920, this once-thriving hotel entered a rapid decline following the Great Depression and a series of catastrophic forest fires nearby. In 1940, it became the Rinehart Clinic, which specialized in the treatment of arthritis. Some think the ghosts here may date to the clinic era, since cries of pain can sometimes be heard. The hotel owners (it was renovated back into a hotel around the 1990s) have also reported the sounds of an antique Victrola in the lobby and ghostly hands on their shoulders. A paranormal team led by author Donna Stewart around 2014 also captured weird video footage of a shadow that appears to be a young boy running back and forth in front of a television left on overnight.

Heathman Hotel

1001 SW BROADWAY, PORTLAND

The beautiful Heathman has an amenity few hotels provide: a well-stocked library filled with books signed by their authors. It also has plenty of ghosts. The most frequent legends relate to the "column rooms" of 1003, 803, and 703 (as well as sometimes other rooms that end in three). The story goes that someone jumped from 1003 and now haunts all the rooms she, or he, passed while falling to their doom. The energy in 1003 is definitely sad, lonely, and heavy. On a less dreadful note, some think members of the Heathman family still hang around to watch over the place. A front desk employee reported hearing the sound of their old safe turning when no one was around, and feeling a tug on his pants leg.

Malheur Butte

ONTARIO

Malheur comes from the French meaning "bad hour," supposedly because some French Canadian fur trappers had their supplies stolen by Native Americans nearby. An inspired imagination could instead link the name to the many legends that surround the place. There are stories of witches who gathered at this extinct volcano over a century ago, and ghostly descendants who carry on their occult rites. People have seen flashes of long, dark robes and heard women laughing ominously. Other stories involve fairies or sprites about the size of small dogs that dart among the rocks. At night, these little shapes seem to glow. A few people have even been followed to their car by a growling voice and heavy footsteps, although they are too frightened to turn around and face their (possibly demonic) pursuers.

Bush House Museum

600 MISSION STREET SE, SALEM

Since the Bush House Museum opened in 1953, people have reported seeing a spectral woman peering out from the top-floor windows and hearing breathless female sobbing. Some think what they're seeing and hearing is Eugenia Bush, the youngest daughter of Asahel Bush, a pioneer Salem publisher and banker. Eugenia had a mental breakdown in the 1890s, and her father sent her to a Boston institution. (Reports that Asahel actually kept Eugenia prisoner in the basement seem far-fetched.) She only returned after her father's death in 1913 when her devoted sister Sally retrieved her so the pair could live out their days together.

Asahel built the house in 1878–1879, equipping it with the best the era had to offer: central heat, hot and cold running water, gaslight fixtures, and ten fireplaces carved from Italian marble. Asahel's children later donated the house and hundred-acre farmstead to Salem for use as a park, and many of the original furnishings from the Bush days remain. Other members of the family may remain too: people report objects sliding along tables, and the shadowy figure of a man in a suit, possibly Asahel himself, fiddling with a pocket watch.

Siletz Bay Phantom Ship

NEAR MO'S RESTAURANT, 860 SW FIFTY-FIRST STREET, LINCOLN CITY

It lasts just a few seconds, but on certain foggy days, a phantom schooner reportedly glides over the surface of Siletz Bay and then disappears. For some, the ship appears in opaque white as if formed from the fog. For others, the vessel looks entirely real, down to seaweed dripping from its anchor.

The story of the phantom ship is linked in local lore to a wreck that happened more than 150 years ago. The story goes that a ship ran aground in Siletz Bay, and by the time locals got there, it was apparently missing both cargo and crew. Some researchers think the ship was the *Blanco*, which wrecked in 1864. Bits of *some* ship did protrude from the bay's sand and mud for years, adding to the legend, before finally disappearing around the 1960s.

Is the phantom ship the *Blanco* or one of the countless other ships that floundered nearby? It's hard to say, but the pier that extends over the beach from Mo's Restaurant is reportedly the best place to try out your ghost-ship goggles.

Yaquina Bay Lighthouse

NEWPORT

The Yaquina Bay Lighthouse operated for only three years in the 1870s before being abandoned. Soon, the structure was decaying and collecting ghostly rumors—tales of eerie noises and the faces of dead lighthouse keepers shining in the mist. There were also reports of a redheaded, skull-faced sailor who often showed up glowering at the base of the lighthouse.

Some have identified the sailor as Evan MacClure, captain of whaling ship the *Moncton*. Legend has it that MacClure and his first mate fought over a woman, and while MacClure won, the first mate later led a mutiny. MacClure was driven into a small boat and set adrift. In January 1874, locals watching a terrible storm at the Devil's Punchbowl saw a boat wash ashore with a redheaded man who had a "face like a skeleton." The man stepped onto the rocks for just a moment before a giant wave washed him away.

The other famous story here is of a beautiful young woman who disappeared at the lighthouse, leaving only a pool of warm blood and a handkerchief. This is a rare case of knowing how the story got started: Lischen M. Miller's (fictional) Gothic tale "The Haunted Light at Newport-by-the-Sea," published in *Pacific Monthly* in 1899.

HAUNTED OREGON EATERIES

The Sparrow Bakery

50 SE SCOTT STREET, BEND

Hungry locals and tourists alike flock here for the breakfast sandwiches, but this bakery is also known for its ghosts. The building used to be an ironworks foundry and payroll office, and long-dead former workers have been blamed for stealing bread, opening and closing doors, and causing loud crashes when no one's around. At least one employee has also heard ghostly giggles.

Old Town Pizza

226 NW DAVIS STREET, PORTLAND

This pizza parlor was once home to the Merchant Hotel. It's said that a sex worker named Nina frequented a basement brothel but met a bad end in an elevator shaft after informing on her pimp. People still feel her, in cold gusts and shivers of sudden unease, or hear her swishing skirts. A few have even seen her appear in a black dress. The name *Nina* is scratched into a brick in a back booth, and has become part of the legend.

Wildflower Grill

4250 NE HIGHWAY 101, LINCOLN CITY

A friendly ghost named Matilda haunts this breakfast and lunch spot. She mostly rattles doorknobs and slams doors but has also been known to pinch the occasional bottom.

Rimsky-Korsakoffee House

707 SE TWELFTH AVENUE, PORTLAND

Named for Russian composer Nikolay Rimsky-Korsakov and filled with an atmosphere best described as "casually threatening," this place is known for its odd happenings as much as for its delicious coffee and desserts. Tables have been reported shaking or rising; one even supposedly went through a wall and reappeared. (It's not quite clear if this is the work of ghosts or just performance art, however.) Strange music has also been reported after dark, possibly played by the wonderfully eccentric owner, Goody Cable.

Gracie's Sea Hag

58 HIGHWAY 101, DEPOE BAY

A local favorite for seafood, this place seems to attract customers so loyal they hang around after death. There are also reports of unusual noises, and some sort of entity that loves to steal the silverware.

McMenamins Cornelius Pass Roadhouse

4045 NE CORNELIUS PASS ROAD, HILLSBORO

Also known as the Imbrie Farm, this place is said to be haunted by the ghost of a boy who fell down the stairs to his death here, although members of the Imbrie family have denied that anything like that ever happened. Employees have reported frigid spots and glasses that shatter without any apparent interference.

Witch's Castle

LOWER MACLEAY TRAIL, FOREST PARK, PORTLAND

Ominous laughter. Screams of fright. Shadowy figures and ghostly lights. All have been reported in Macleay Park after dark, the supposed remnants of a battle between two families that still plays out in spectral form.

The stories center on the mossy ruins of a stone structure known as the Witch's Castle. In the 1850s, a man named Danford Balch owned a cabin nearby on hundreds of acres. He hired a worker named Mortimer Stump to help clear the land, and before long, Stump and Balch's eldest daughter, Anna, fell in love. They eloped, but Balch disapproved of the union. After an argument with Stump and his family, Balch shot the young man in the face.

The stone ruins are not, however, the remains of the Balch cabin, nor where he was subsequently hanged. They are a former ranger station and restroom. As for the ghosts? You'll have to decide for yourself if they're real, although be warned that some who venture into the park at night never return.

Oaks Amusement Park

7805 SE OAKS PARK WAY, PORTLAND

The Oaks is one of the nation's oldest continually operating amusement parks. After opening in 1905 to capitalize on traffic from the Lewis and Clark Exposition, the park became such a smashing success it was dubbed the Coney Island of the Northwest. Visitors were thrilled by the giant Ferris wheel, beautiful carousel, and nightly fireworks.

Such a happy place may not seem a likely candidate for hauntings, but a few sad spirits reportedly linger. Several people have seen a young girl standing quietly near the carousel or picnic area, wearing 1920s or '30s clothing with a big white bow in her hair. Employees have also heard little-girl sobs after dark or footsteps following them. Others have seen a twentysomething man who appears in shades of gray and looks lost. He may be the ghost of David Smith, said to have died in a streetcar accident at the park in the early twentieth century. The little girl, meanwhile, is rumored to be the ghost of a child who fell and died near the entrance. She grips people by the elbow, looking for someone to guide her into the park she never got to experience in life.

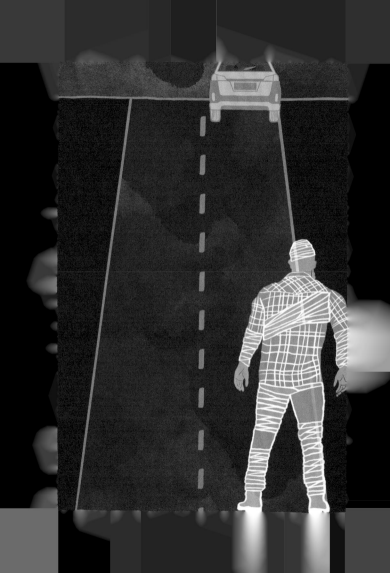

Bandage Man

**HIGHWAY 101 AT HIGHWAY 26,
NEAR CANNON BEACH**

Be careful driving on stormy nights near the intersection of Highways 101 and 26 near Cannon Beach. Be especially careful if you're driving a pickup truck. For decades, people have reported a figure in bloodied bandages who jumps into the back of their trucks and lunges at them. Those who survive the encounter say he leaves strips of bandages behind that smell like rotting meat.

Bandage Man is a uniquely Oregonian home-brewed blend of a ghost, monster, cryptid, and possibly alien, depending on the telling. Earlier stories describe him as a huge lumberjack who was injured in a logging accident and escaped from his ambulance when it was caught in a landslide. Whether he attacks as a living murderer or a ghost bent on revenge (or a sasquatch or a survivor of a crashed spaceship) is unclear. Regardless, those in the know avoid the area at night, just to be safe.

McMenamins Edgefield

2126 SW HALSEY STREET, TROUTDALE

Today these seventy-four acres are home to a hotel, a winery, a golf course, restaurants, and more, but the buildings began in 1911 as the Multnomah County Poor Farm. Hundreds of people who couldn't support themselves lived and worked on the farm. In later years, the site became a home for children with psychological issues, a tuberculosis hospital, and a nursing home. It was abandoned in 1982 before the McMenamins bought the place and transformed it into its present glory.

Paranormal researchers say the property may have more ghosts per acre than anywhere in Oregon. There's a large ghost dog who nuzzles guests from their sleep but disappears when people call the front desk to complain. There's a man in a butcher's apron, a little girl who calls out nursery rhymes at night, a woman in white, and a phantasmic little boy (the latter two are known to peer into first-floor windows). One security guard even saw a kitchen knife sail through the air and embed itself in a wall—possibly the handiwork of a former circus performer who spent her final days at the facility.

Knight Hall, Pacific University

2204 COLLEGE WAY, FOREST GROVE

Tales of a haunting at Knight Hall, now Pacific University's Admissions Department, go back decades. One of the most famous stories dates to 1971 when a watchman locking up for the evening heard singing from the third floor. When he went upstairs to check things out, he saw a woman's shape enveloped in glimmering blue light. He never went back alone.

The ghost has a name: Vera. In 1969, students holding a seance received a message identifying the ghost as Vera Herrick, a student from the 1880s whose father, Reverend John Herrick, was the school's president. Subsequent research verified that the reverend was president at the time but he didn't have a daughter named Vera. A later seance suggested that Vera was murdered by gunshot, but again, there are no corroborating reports.

That doesn't matter to people who've worked in Knight Hall and swear there's a ghost. They've seen doors open and close on their own, watched heavy objects slide along the floor, and smelled a scent like burning insects fill the air.

HAUNTED OREGON SCHOOLS

South Eugene High School

400 E NINETEENTH AVENUE, EUGENE

Around 1958, student Robert Turnbull Grankey was working as a stagehand in the auditorium when he slipped in the catwalks and fell to his death. (Supposedly, the seats he landed on had dents for years, until they were replaced in 1994 to quell superstition.) Students and staff have seen a translucent figure in the catwalks, and heard footsteps, creaking, and whispered dialogue when no one was around. Some have even seen a figure standing in the balcony or at the back of the auditorium, but upon closer inspection the figure vanishes.

Lane Community College

4000 E THIRTIETH AVENUE, EUGENE

Eugene may have the corner on haunted schools—and at Lane Community College, it's the elevator that gets all the attention. It's said that a janitor died there in the 1960s from either a fall or from being crushed. There are no newspaper reports to corroborate this, yet people report hearing moans, sobs, and cries for help in the elevator that goes to the first two floors of the Center Building.

Oregon State University

1500 SW JEFFERSON WAY, CORVALLIS

Waldo Hall, which opened in 1907 as the women's dorm, may be haunted by the ghost of Ida Kidder, the school's first librarian, who died in her room there in 1920. Nicknamed "Mother Kidder," she was so spunky and beloved that she was laid in state in the library after her death. Odd noises, music, and strange figures have all been seen here, although some might be explained by the old pipes—or by a (living) woman who was secretly living in the building at night for a time.

The Lodge at Hot Lake Springs

66172 OR-203, LA GRANDE

Some hauntings are defined by what people see. Others, by what they smell or feel. The hauntings at Hot Lake are marked by what people hear.

The first Hot Lake Hotel was built in 1864, and by the 1920s, it was a prominent health resort. Guests came to enjoy fine dining and lodging, to relax in the mineral waters, and to undergo treatments offered by Dr. William Phy. The resort began its decline in the 1930s, and the building later served as a WWII flight school, a nursing home, and a restaurant before being restored to its use as a hotel. Yet the past seems to have stuck around.

In the 1970s, a caretaker reported that he often heard a woman screaming in a former surgery room on the third floor. Then there's the piano: purchased for the original hotel and reportedly once owned by Robert E. Lee's in-laws, it plays all by itself. Visitors have also heard rocking chairs move on their own or experienced the creaking sound of wheels going up and down, up and down empty wheelchair ramps.

Resources

Where, and How, to Find Ghosts

Need even more ghosts than the ones mentioned in this book? Beyond guidebooks, TV shows, and Google, there are a variety of other places to start hunting. Try talking to elders in your community or reaching out to local historians or historical societies. Local newspaper archives can be a treasure trove, and many are now digitized (try your library or Newspapers.com).

Search for stories not just of ghosts or hauntings but murders, suicides, accidents, tragic deaths, or tales of deep devotion—anything that might cause a spirit to hang around. If there's a particularly old hotel, theater, or B&B nearby, that's often a good place to start looking. Guided tours of historical sites can be helpful, although some places are reluctant to talk about their ghosts. Ghost walks, haunted history tours, and cemetery tours are also great starting points, but be aware that guides vary greatly in their commitment to facts versus legends.

Once you've identified a potential haunted hot spot, try to visit when it's quiet (but never trespass, of course). While some people enjoy assembling advanced gear, you might start out with basic audio- and video-recording equipment, a flashlight, and trigger objects—a doll, cards, Scrabble tiles, or coins, which may be able to provoke a reaction from a spirit. Experiment with taking photos in low ambient light, which may include infrared film or night-vision settings. Audio-recording equipment may allow you to capture electronic voice phenomena (sounds human ears can't usually pick up but which can be heard upon playback). Try asking questions of the ghost, like, "What is your name?" or "Why are you here?" and listen carefully to the audio after the investigation. Check photos and video for anomalies, though be aware that many a speck of dust and camera strap has been mistaken for a ghost. Leave the trigger objects in a room where no one has access, then check back later to see if they've moved. You might be surprised by what you find.

Whatever you do, be patient. Ghosts don't perform on command, and it may take several visits for anything strange to happen. If it does, be grateful and try to document it, but don't push your luck by staying around longer than you're wanted. If you get a strong sense to leave, do so.

What to Do If You Think You're Haunted

Keep in mind that many, if not most, seemingly paranormal experiences have banal explanations: rodents, mold, faulty heating or cooling systems, voices carried across water, or even low-frequency vibrations that can cause dread and hallucinations. If you're having repeated issues, try simply asking the ghost to stop acting up (this can be surprisingly effective). You may want to contact one of the paranormal groups listed on page 127, many of which offer investigation services for those in distress. But be cautious: research such groups beforehand, asking about their methods and goals. You shouldn't be asked to pay for services, particularly if the group wants to come back multiple times.

Further Reading

Ghost Hunter's Guide to Portland and the Oregon Coast
by Jeff Dwyer

Ghost Stories from the Pacific Northwest
by Margaret Read MacDonald

Ghosthunting Oregon by Donna Stewart

Ghostland: An American History in Haunted Places
by Colin Dickey

Ghosts, Critters, & Sacred Places of Washington and Oregon by Jefferson Davis

Ghosts of Seattle by Athena

Phantom Past, Indigenous Presence: Native Ghosts in North American Culture and History edited by Colleen E. Boyd and Coll Thrush

Spooked in Seattle: A Haunted Handbook by Ross Allison

Washington's Haunted Hotspots by Linda Moffitt

Weird Oregon by Jeff Davis and Al Eufrasio

Weird Washington by Jeff Davis and Al Eufrasio

Ghost Tours & Experiences

Note: These listings were compiled in early 2021 during the COVID–19 pandemic. Check websites for details and availability.

Washington

Bill Speidel's Underground Tour: UndergroundTour.com | Seattle's long-running underground tour, with a "hands-on, lights-off" Underground Paranormal Experience available.

Friday Harbor Ghost Walks: HistoricFridayHarbor.org | Historic tours are offered in May and October.

Gore & Lore Tours: BellingHistory.com | A guide in period costume covers the creepier side of Bellingham in a one-hour tour; options available for downtown and historic Fairhaven.

The Grit City Ghost Tour: PrettyGrittyTours.com | One-hour paranormal walking tours through downtown Tacoma.

Haunted Histories & Mysteries of Port Townsend: PTMain-Street.org/haunted-histories-mysteries-of-port-townsend | A weekend of ghostly activities on the historic waterfront planned each year around Halloween.

Port Gamble Ghost Walk: PortGambleParanormal.com | Three-hour tours of the museum, cemetery, famed Walker-Ames House, and more.

Spirit Tales Tours: GhostsAndCritters.com/ghost%20walks .html | Local ghost and folklore expert Jeff Davis presents tours in collaboration with the Clark County History Museum.

Spooked in Seattle Tours: SpookedInSeattle.com | Created in 2004 by Ross Allison, paranormal investigator and founder of AGHOST (Advanced Ghost Hunters of Seattle-Tacoma); features both tours and ghost hunts.

Oregon

Astoria Ghost Tour: AstoriaGhostTour.com | Forty-five-minute weekend tours that combine Astoria's history with paranormal investigations.

Beyond Bizarre Ghost Tour: PortlandWalkingTours.com/tours/beyond-bizarre-ghost-tour | Handle ghost-hunting gear and explore the darker, seamier side of Portland; includes a hunt for the legendary ghost of the working girl Nina.

Ghosts and Legends of the Oregon Coast: HauntedTaft.com | Hear about the Siletz Bay phantom schooner and the oldest tavern on the coast during this walking tour of the Taft District of Lincoln City.

Historical Haunts of Downtown Bend: DeschutesHistory.org | One-hour walking tours through historic downtown Bend offered through the Deschutes Historical Museum, with a "pinch of the paranormal."

Northwest Ghost Tours: NWGhostTours.com | Tours in Oregon City and Seaside, Oregon, by local historian and paranormal investigator Rocky Smith.

Oregon Ghost Conference: OregonGhostConference.com | A week of paranormal classes, tours, and events on the Oregon coast.

Portland Ghosts: PortlandGhosts.com | Learn about shanghai-ing and the legends of the underground tunnels in this roughly one-hour tour of downtown Portland.

Shanghai Tunnels/Portland Underground: PortlandTunnels.com | All about the legends of the Shanghai Tunnels, with a special ghost tour among the offerings.

Selected Paranormal Groups in the Pacific Northwest

ADVANCED GHOST HUNTERS OF SEATTLE-TACOMA (AGHOST) | AGHOST.ORG

CASCADIA PARANORMAL INVESTIGATIONS | FACEBOOK.COM /CASCADIAPARANORMAL

CENTRAL OREGON PARANORMAL | CENTRALORPARANORMAL.WIXSITE.COM /CENTRALORPARANORMAL

DON'T PANIC PARANORMAL | DONTPANICPARANORMAL.COM

OLYMPIC PENINSULA PARANORMAL SOCIETY | OLYMPICPENINSULAPARANORMALSOCIETY.COM

OREGON PARANORMAL | OREGONPARANORMAL.COM

PUGET SOUND GHOST HUNTERS | PSGHOSTHUNTERS.COM

SHADOW KEEPERS | SHADOWKEEPERS.ORG

WASHINGTON STATE PARANORMAL INVESTIGATIONS AND RESEARCH (WSPIR) | WSPIR.COM

Index

About the Author

BESS LOVEJOY is the author of *Rest in Pieces: The Curious Fates of Famous Corpses*. She is a former editor on the Schott's Almanac book series, as well as on the Mental Floss and *Smithsonian* magazine websites. Her writing has appeared in the *New York Times*, the *Boston Globe*, *Lapham's Quarterly*, The Public Domain Review, Atlas Obscura, and elsewhere. She is a fifth-generation Pacific Northwesterner and currently resides in West Seattle. She's never seen a ghost but loves the region's haunted history.

About the Illustrator

ANARACHEL HUMPHREY is a designer and illustrator based out of Brooklyn, New York. Hailing from Spokane, Washington, she grew up between families both in the Pacific Northwest and Brazil. She is inspired by her changing surroundings and developed a fascination early on for the in-between and the transient. To see more of Anarachel's work, visit her Instagram @anarachelism, or find her online at Anarachelism.com.